yukismart.com/b/649e36

apple

яблуко
iabluko

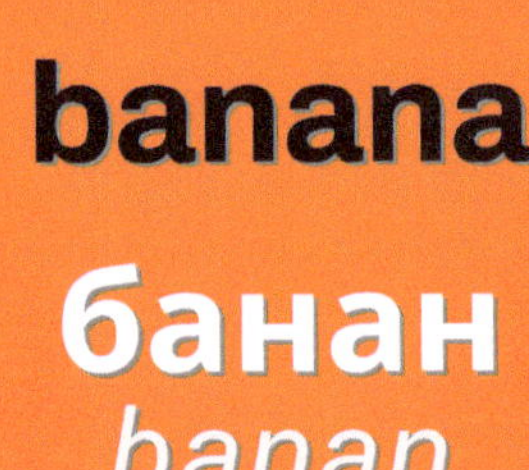

banana

банан
banan

pear

груша
hrusha

cherry

вишня
vyshnia

lime

лайм
laim

lemon

лимон
lymon

quince

айва
aiva

kiwi

ківі
kivi

grapes

виноград
vynohrad

watermelon

кавун
kavun

orange

апельсин
apelsyn

clementine

клементин
klementyn

strawberry

полуниця
polunytsia

raspberry

малина
malyna

cranberry

журавлина
zhuravlyna

blueberry

чорниця
chornytsia

currant

смородина
smorodyna

blackberry

ожина
ozhyna

juice

сік
sik

jam

варення
varennia

toast

тост
tost

grapefruit

грейпфрут
hreipfrut

melon

диня
dynia

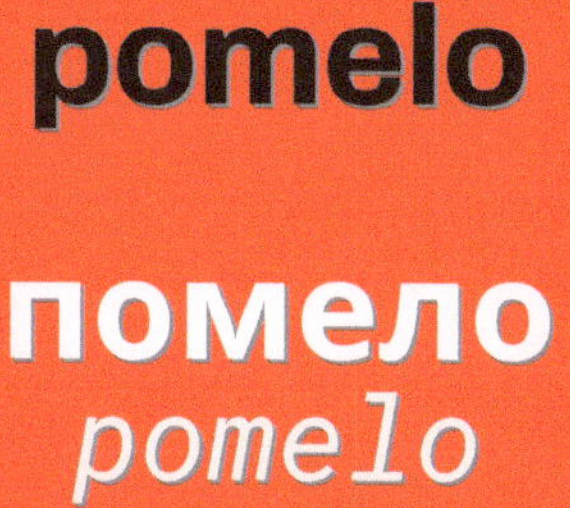

pomelo

помело
pomelo

kumquat

кумкват
kumkvat

mirabelle plum

мірабель
mirabel

peach

персик
persyk

apricot

абрикос
abrykos

plum

слива
slyva

pineapple

ананас
ananas

pomegranate

гранат
hranat

olive

оливка
olyvka

fig

інжир
inzhyr

date

фінік
finik

avocado

авокадо
avokado

lychee

лічі
lichi

persimmon

хурма
khurma

star fruit

карамболь
karambol

mango

манго
manho

rambutan

рамбутан
rambutan

longan

лонган
lonhan

langsat

лангсат
lanhsat

mangosteen

мангостан
manhostan

jackfruit

джекфрут
dzhekfrut

sapodilla

саподіла
sapodila

guava

гуава
huava

jujube

ююба
iuiuba

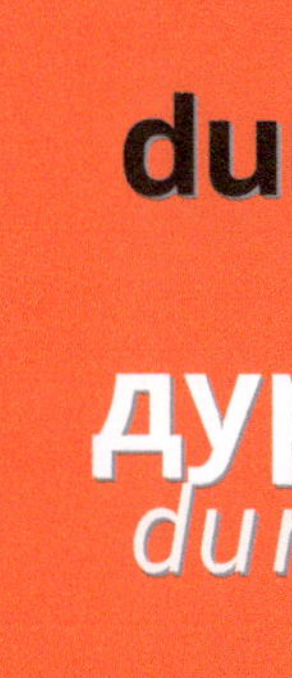

durian

дуріан
durian

soursop

соу-сеп
sou-sep

papaya

папайя
papaiia

dragon fruit

пітая
pitaia

coconut

кокосовий горіх
kokosovyi horikh

cocoa

какао
kakao

chocolate

шоколад
shokolad

potato

картопля
kartoplia

corn

кукурудза
kukurudza

sweet potato

Коренеплоди батату
Koreneplody batatu

pumpkin

гарбуз
harbuz

butternut squash

гарбуз мускатний
harbuz muskatnyi

cassava

маніок
maniok

carrot

морква
morkva

tomato

помідор
pomidor

mushroom

гриб
hryb

broccoli

броколі
brokoli

asparagus

спаржа
sparzha

artichoke

артишок
artyshok

cucumber

огірок
ohirok

spinach

шпинат
shpynat

cauliflower

цвітна капуста
tsvitna kapusta

zucchini

Кабачок-цукіні
Kabachok-tsukini

lettuce

салат-латук

salat-latuk

cabbage

капуста

kapusta

eggplant

баклажан
baklazhan

turnip

ріпа
ripa

radish

редиска
redyska

beet

буряк
buriak

rhubarb

ревінь
revin

Brussel sprout

Брюссельська капуста
Briusselska kapusta

leek

цибуля-порей
tsybulia-porei

mint

м'ята

m'iata

celeriac

корінь селери

korin selery

endive

цикорій салатний

tsykorii salatnyi

celery

селера

selera

peas

горошинки
horoshynky

chickpeas

нут
nut

green bean

стручкова квасоля

struchkova kvasolia

red bean

червона квасоля

chervona kvasolia

mung bean

паростки квасолі мунго

parostky kvasoli munho

fennel

фенхель
fenkhel

parsnip

пастернак
pasternak

bell pepper

болгарський перець

bolharskyi perets

chili pepper

перець чилі

perets chyli

pepper

перець

perets

onion

цибуля
tsybulia

garlic

часник
chasnyk

ginger

імбир
imbyr

macadamia

макадамія
makadamiia

pecans

горіхи пекан
horikhy pekan

cashew

кеш'ю
kesh'iu

hazelnuts

фундук
funduk

almond

мигдаль
myhdal

pistachio

фісташки
fistashky

peanut

арахіс
arakhis

chestnut

каштан
kashtan

walnuts

волоські горіхи
voloski horikhy